Classics of
The Royal Ballet

Classics of
The Royal Ballet
Jesse Davis
Introductions by Mary Clarke
COWARD, McCANN & GEOGHEGAN, INC.
NEW YORK

For my dear Mother

Library of Congress Cataloging in Publication Data

Davis, Jesse
Classics of the Royal Ballet
SUMMARY: The plots of six ballets are accompanied by
photographs of performances by the Royal Ballet.
Included are "The Nutcracker," "Swan Lake," "La Fille
Mal Gardée," "Giselle," "Romeo and Juliet," and "The
Sleeping Beauty."
1. Royal Ballet.   2. Ballets—Stories, plots, etc.
[1. Royal Ballet.   2. Ballets—Stories, plots, etc.]
I. Clarke, Mary, date.   II. Title.
GV1786.R6D28   792.8′4   79-10866
ISBN 0-698-20502-2

Printed in the United States of America

Designed by Paul Chevannes

Contents

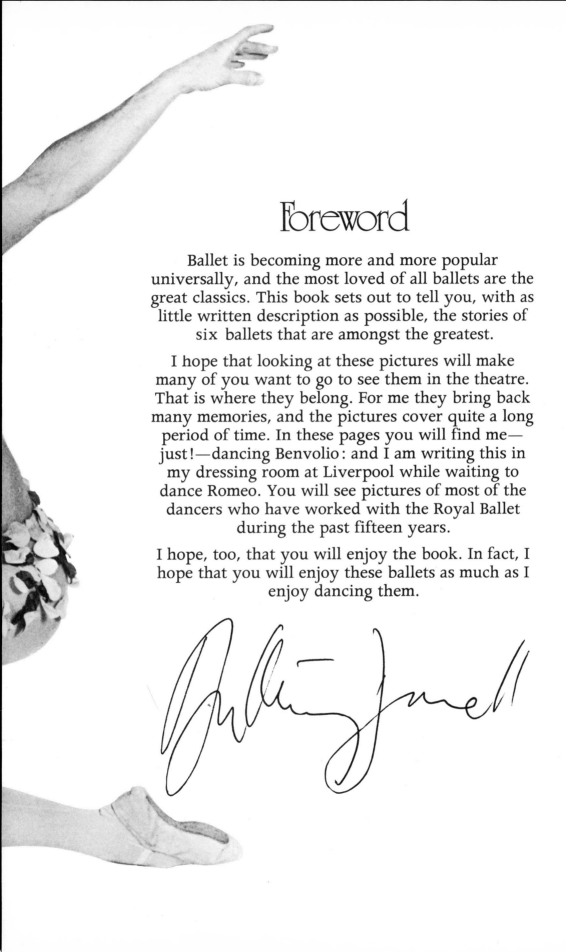

Foreword

Ballet is becoming more and more popular universally, and the most loved of all ballets are the great classics. This book sets out to tell you, with as little written description as possible, the stories of six ballets that are amongst the greatest.

I hope that looking at these pictures will make many of you want to go to see them in the theatre. That is where they belong. For me they bring back many memories, and the pictures cover quite a long period of time. In these pages you will find me— just!—dancing Benvolio: and I am writing this in my dressing room at Liverpool while waiting to dance Romeo. You will see pictures of most of the dancers who have worked with the Royal Ballet during the past fifteen years.

I hope, too, that you will enjoy the book. In fact, I hope that you will enjoy these ballets as much as I enjoy dancing them.

The Nutcracker

Choreography & Production: *Rudolf Nureyev*. Music: *Pyotr Ilyich Tchaikovsky*.
Designs: *Nicholas Georgiadis*.

Cast. Clara: *Merle Park*. Herr Drosselmeyer/The Prince: *Rudolf Nureyev*.

Dr. Stahlbaum: *David Drew*. Frau Stahlbaum: *Rosalind Eyre*. Fritz: *Stephen Beagley*.
Louisa: *Ann Jenner*. Grandmother: *Gerd Larsen*. Grandfather: *Ronald Emblen*.
The Nutcracker: *Paul Benson*. The Rat King: *William Perrie*. Snowflakes: *Laura Connor, Vergie Derman*.
Spanish Dance: *Ann Jenner, Stephen Beagley*. Arab Dance: *Gerd Larsen, Ronald Emblen, Vergie Derman, Michael Batchelor*. Chinese Dance: *Wayne Eagling, Mark Silver, Graham Fletcher*.
Russian Dance: *Rosalind Eyre, David Drew*. Pastorale: *Lesley Collier, Alfreda Thorogood, Michael Coleman*.

The Nutcracker (original French title, *Casse Noisette*) was the last of three great ballet scores to be written by Pyotr Ilyich Tchaikovsky (1840–1893) for the Imperial Russian Ballet at the end of the nineteenth century. The other two were *Swan Lake* and *The Sleeping Beauty* and they are today among the most popular works in the whole ballet repertory. *The Nutcracker*, which has become a traditional Christmas entertainment in Britain and throughout the United States, was not, alas, a success when first produced at the famous Maryinsky Theatre in St. Petersburg on 18 December 1892. The ballet master and principal choreographer in St. Petersburg at that time was the Frenchman, Marius Petipa. He had worked with Tchaikovsky on *The Sleeping Beauty* and his method was to prepare for the composer a very detailed scenario, asking for a precise number of bars of music for the different scenes and dances. He wrote the scenario for *The Nutcracker* and gave it to Tchaikovsky but then fell ill and the production was staged by his assistant, Lev Ivanov (1834–1901) who, subsequently, was responsible for the 'white' or lakeside scenes in *Swan Lake*. Tchaikovsky did not like the task, especially the job of writing the music for the 'sweetmeats' divertissement in Act II. But he wrote some of his most enchanting music for the first act of the ballet and his genius shone also in the great *pas de deux* at the end.

The Nutcracker was first staged in London by the then Vic-Wells (now Royal) Ballet in 1934 and was re-created from the original St. Petersburg version by Nicholai Sergueyev who had been in charge of the ballets there before the Revolution. The Sugar Plum Fairy was danced by Alicia Markova and when she and Anton Dolin founded their own company they also presented this version and later danced it with Festival Ballet. Not until 1968 did the Royal Ballet put on a *Nutcracker* at Covent Garden and they asked Rudolf Nureyev to stage it. He did an entirely new version in which Clara's dream becomes more like a nightmare but Clara becomes the ballerina rôle and Drosselmeyer turns into her Prince. Nureyev and Merle Park danced the first performance (shown in the following pages) but Antoinette Sibley and Jennifer Penney were enchanting Claras and both Anthony Dowell and David Wall danced as Drosselmeyer/Prince. The ballet was magnificently designed by Nicholas Georgiadis.

Act I

It is Christmas Eve early in the nineteenth century. The wealthy Mayor, Dr. Stahlbaum, is giving a party for his son and daughters, Fritz, Louisa and Clara, his friends and their children. The children play delightedly with the presents they have just received, the boys with soldiers and hobby horses and the girls with dolls. Their games are interrupted by the arrival of old Herr Drosselmeyer who enters the room swathed in a dark, voluminous cloak. His strange antics and mysterious air fascinate, and half frighten, the boys and girls. The party progresses and the ballroom fills with music.

The guests perform elegant dances beneath the glittering chandeliers. But, before long, the children are up to new mischief and the graceful swirls and delicate music are halted when they play tricks on their startled, but amused, parents.

Then Herr Drosselmeyer intervenes. To occupy the children, he brings out fantastic mechanical toys: a soldier, a Turk and a pretty doll, and, with a wave of his hand, makes them dance before the amazed and delighted guests. As the wondrously life-like automatons stop moving, the children creep gingerly forward and, hesitantly, touch them, not quite sure if they are real or not and, at first, more than half afraid of them. But they are just toys after all.

Herr Drosselmeyer produces a special present for Clara, a Nutcracker in the form of a soldier.

She is delighted, but her brother Fritz is jealous and he snatches the toy and breaks it. Clara bursts into tears, but Herr Drosselmeyer easily repairs the Nutcracker and restores it to the weeping Clara. Delighted, Clara dances with the toy, her tears quickly forgotten.

The guests take the floor again, this time led by the Stahlbaums' grandparents, who, after a brave try, find the energetic dancing a little too much for them. After all the excitement of the party, Clara is exhausted and soon falls into a deep sleep. Clara's rest, however, is uneasy and her dreams are invaded by rats who do battle with the toy soldiers who have come to life.

The battle sways to and fro, and just as the King Rat is gaining the upper hand, Clara fells him with a well-aimed candle.

Clara rescues her beloved Nutcracker from the battlefield and, all at once, he turns into a handsome Prince and dances a *pas de deux* with her.

The Nutcracker Prince whisks Clara away to a wondrous Kingdom of Snow where they watch the glittering Dance of the Snowflakes.

Act II

Then Clara finds herself alone once more in the ballroom, besieged by grotesque and terrifying dolls, but the Prince appears again and banishes the frightening apparitions. Clara's dolls come to life and dance *divertissements* for her entertainment, beginning with two Spanish dolls who perform a spirited, exciting, *Danse Espangnole*.

A trio of exotic Chinese dolls perform an unusual acrobatic dance to a flute accompaniment. Then three dancers in a pastorale *pas de trois* delight Clara with their grace and beauty. The exquisite *Valse des Fleurs* brings the entertainment to a glorious conclusion.

Clara, now transformed into a beautiful Fairy Queen, partners the handsome Nutcracker Prince in a *grand pas de deux*.

The culmination of all Clara's dreams realised, and the store of her imagination exhausted, the exquisite *pas de deux* draws to a close. Clara's dancing toys, including her Spanish and Arabian dolls parade briefly once more through her dreams. Suddenly, she wakes. The party is over and the guests are leaving. As she gazes from the door, still clutching her Nutcracker, she sees Herr Drosselmeyer's form gradually veiled by the falling snow as he vanishes into the night.

Swan Lake

Choreography: *Marius Petipa & Lev Ivanov*. Produced by: *Nicolai Sergueyev* (with revisions by *Ninette de Valois*). Music: *Pyotr Ilyich Tchaikovsky*. Designs: *Leslie Hurry*

Cast. Odette/Odile: *Merle Park*. Prince Siegfried: *Anthony Dowell*. Queen Mother: *Gerd Larsen*. Von Rothbart: *Derek Rencher*.
Tutor: *Garry Grant*. Master of Ceremonies: *Leslie Edwards*. Peasant Girl: *Christine Woodward*. Pas de Trois: *Ann Jenner, Alfreda Thorogood, Michael Coleman*. Waltz: *Jacqui Tallis, Sandra Conley, Judith Howe, Sally Inkin, Hilary Tickner, Wendy Ellis, Mark Silver, Michael Corder, Christopher Carr, Michael Batchelor, Stephen Beagley, Ross MacGibbon*. Four Swans: *Judith Howe, Pippa Wylde, Marguerite Porter, Wendy Groombridge*. Cygnets: *Susan Lockwood, Barbara Lower, Belinda Corken, Anita Young*. Pas de Quatre: *Wendy Ellis, Marguerite Porter, Michael Batchelor, Michael Corder*. Spanish: *Rosalind Eyre, Jacqui Tallis, David Drew, Ross MacGibbon*. Neapolitan: *Lesley Collier, Wayne Sleep*.

Swan Lake is today the most famous ballet in the world and it is performed everywhere. Yet the first production in Moscow in 1877 was not a success. Two years earlier the Director of the Bolshoy Theatre, V. P. Begichev, commissioned Tchaikovsky to compose the score for a ballet based on a libretto by Begichev and Vasily Geltzer. In doing so Tchaikovsky tried to raise the level of ballet music (and did so) but the score was misunderstood, described as 'too symphonic' and interpolations were made. The choreography, by Wenzel Reisinger (1827–1892), was undistinguished and he gave the rôle of Odette-Odile to his favourite ballerina, Pelageia Karpakova, noted for her beauty rather than her dancing. The ballet stayed in the Moscow repertory, in different stagings by Joseph Hansen in 1880 and 1882, but it was not until 27 January 1895 that Tchaikovsky's ballet found its true realisation. On that date (after the composer's death), it was restaged with the French title *Le Lac des Cygnes* at the Maryinsky Theatre in St. Petersburg, supervised by Marius Petipa, who arranged the choreography for the first and third acts, assisted by Lev Ivanov who is credited with the choreography for the lakeside acts – the second and fourth. The role of Odette-Odile was, in this version, created by the Italian virtuoso ballerina Pierina Legnani who introduced the famous and difficult 32 fouettés into the ballroom scene. This version, taught to them in 1934 by Nicolai Sergueyev, has always been the base for the Royal Ballet's stagings and the production they have today probably resembles the St. Petersburg one as closely as any. (The Russians have constantly revised the ballet and in the West choreographers and producers have tried all sorts of different approaches, none of them improving on the traditional choreography).

The success of *Swan Lake* is ensured by Tchaikovsky's hauntingly beautiful score, by the romantic and tragic story, and by the superb choreography devised by Petipa and Ivanov. There are two great *pas de deux*, the lyric one that celebrates the love of Odette and Siegfried in Act II, and the dazzling one for Odile and Siegfried in Act III. The patterns for the 'swan' dances by the corps de ballet are poetic and testimony to Ivanov's sensitive approach. The Royal Ballet version also includes the brilliant Neapolitan Dance and *pas de quatre* by Frederick Ashton for Act III.

In 1934, Alicia Markova danced Odette-Odile partnered by Robert Helpmann. She was succeeded by Margot Fonteyn, the greatest interpreter of the rôle in English ballet. Svetlana Beriosova and Natalya Makarova have shone in *Swan Lake*. In recent years the Prince's rôle (created in 1895 by the elderly Pavel Gerdt) has been enlarged to give him more dancing. With the Royal Ballet, Nureyev, Dowell, Wall and Baryshnikov all give magnificent performances.

Act I

It is Prince Siegfried's twenty-first birthday. His friends and the peasant boys and girls, have gathered in the palace gardens to celebrate. Siegfried's young courtiers dance exuberantly for their Prince amid the general merrymaking. Trumpets ring out, heralding the arrival of Siegfried's mother, the Queen.

Knowing her son's love of hunting, the Queen gives Siegfried a crossbow. At the same time she reminds him that now he is of age he must marry, to which end she will present six eligible young girls to him at a ball the next night. With the prospect of a royal marriage and Siegfried's birthday to inspire them, the guests recommence their festivities with a lively *pas de trois* danced by two girls and a boy. As evening draws on and the guests depart a strange melancholy descends on Siegfried, who is left alone, brooding on his mother's words.

Act II

Siegfried's reflections are interrupted by his friends who have seen a flight of swans and urge the Prince to come hunting with them. Siegfried is fascinated by the beauty of the swans in flight and follows the party to a lakeside where the hunters will lie in wait. The Prince, however, wishes to watch the swans alone and tells his fellows to leave. Suddenly, a lone swan settles on the lake and changes into a beautiful girl wearing a crown. Siegfried comes out of hiding and shows the frightened maiden that he means her no harm, but has fallen under the spell of her beauty. Reassured, the maiden tells Siegfried of her plight. She is Odette, a Princess, whom the evil magician, Von Rothbart, has bewitched and made Queen of the Swan Maidens. She may take her human form only in the hours of darkness. The spell can be broken if a Prince falls in love with her and vows to be faithful to her alone for ever.

As Odette tells Siegfried this, Von Rothbart appears and glories in his power over the helpless swan maidens. The Prince thinks to free them by killing Von Rothbart with an arrow from his crossbow. But Odette knows that the evil magician cannot be injured in this way and prevents him. Together they flee the lakeside and Von Rothbart retires, victorious. The hunters return and are about to shoot at the swan maidens when Siegfried rushes in and orders them to lower their bows and depart. The Prince turns once more to reassure Odette who stands, arms outspread, before her defenceless charges.

Having banished Odette's fears, Siegfried dances a beautiful *pas de deux* with the enchanted Swan Queen. As they dance together Siegfried and Odette feel their emotions for each other growing stronger and deeper. The Prince and the Swan Queen have fallen in love and their happiness is shown in the tenderness of their dancing.

Four cygnets enter and dance a *pas de quatre* in celebration of Odette's new-found love. But with the dawn the maidens must again take the form of swans and Odette sadly bids Siegfried farewell, changes once more into a swan and flies away, leaving the Prince gazing into the sky.

Trumpets sound unexpectedly, and Von Rothbart, disguised as a nobleman, enters with his daughter, Odile, who, though clad in black, has taken on the appearance of Odette, the Swan Queen. The Prince, totally deceived, is overjoyed and leads Odile away as the next *divertissement*, a Spanish dance, begins. After the Spaniards with their swirling skirts and castanets, come Hungarian dancers with their rich red costumes and imperious bearing. As the entertainment draws to a close, the unsuspecting Prince dances with the bewitching Odile, convinced that she is in reality his beloved Odette.

While they are dancing, Odette appears at the ballroom window, fluttering pitifully in an attempt to warn Siegfried of Odile's deceit. Catching sight of her, Von Rothbart casts a spell over the entire court so that they are blind to her. Prompted by her evil father, whose spell holds Siegfried and the whole court in his sway, Odile continues to masquerade as Odette. By now the combined powers of Von Rothbart and Odile have completely won over the Prince, and as they dance their duet he falls prey to Odile's charms.

As the *pas de deux* ends Siegfried asks Odile to marry him and, thinking to break Von Rothbart's curse, he vows eternal fidelity. The die is cast and Von Rothbart and Odile mockingly reveal their true identities and exit, leaving Siegfried with the grim realisation that he has condemned Odette to perpetual enslavement to the evil Von Rothbart's spell.

Act IV

At the lakeside the faithful swan maidens are anxiously awaiting their Queen's return from the ball. Odette enters heartbroken at what she has seen through the window. She is soon followed by Siegfried seeking Odette amongst her protective swan maidens. He begs her forgiveness telling her of Von Rothbart's deception. Odette forgives Siegfried and tells him that the only way now to escape the spell is for her to drown herself. Siegfried vows to join her.

Von Rothbart appears and tries to no avail, to exercise his power over Odette. The strength and purity of Odette and Siegfried's love overcome his evil and he is cast down. As the lovers throw themselves into the lake, the spell is broken and Von Rothbart dies, freeing the swan maidens and leaving Odette and Siegfried happily reunited in spirit.

La Fille Mal Gardée

Choreography: *Frederick Ashton*. Music: *Ferdinand Hérold and John Lanchbery*.
Designs: *Osbert Lancaster*.

Cast. Widow Simone: *Ronald Emblen*. Lise: *Brenda Last*. Colas: *Desmond Kelly*.
Thomas: *John Auld*. Alain: *David Morse*.

Harvesters: *Artists of the Sadler's Wells Royal Ballet*

The first ballet with the title *La Fille mal gardée* (literally translated – the badly guarded daughter) was staged in France on 1 July 1789 at the Grand Théâtre, Bordeaux. The choreographer was Jean Dauberval (1742–1806), a great innovator in ballet's history. Until that time the subject matter for ballets had been mostly heroic fables or mythological subjects, but Dauberval decided to make his about real people such as inhabited the French countryside in which he worked. Since Dauberval's first version, ballets about *La Fille mal gardée* have been staged throughout Europe and America and have always been a success. The story of true love triumphing over a marriage for money is one that touches all hearts, and the country setting ensures a warm humanity.

In 1959 Frederick Ashton, founder choreographer of the Royal Ballet, decided to do his own version of the ballet. He copied out Dauberval's original libretto in the British Museum and then devised his own treatment of the plot. He also consulted the great Russian ballerina Tamara Karsavina (b. 1885) and learned from her the touching little mime scene in Act II in which Lise dreams of marriage and children. The music for the 1789 version had been a hotch potch taken from popular works by various composers. Ashton asked John Lanchbery, the conductor, to arrange a new score for him, taking as a base that composed by Ferdinand Hérold for a Paris staging in 1828, but inserting a great deal of new material. Lanchbery wrote much of the first act music himself, including the *pas de deux*, the comic solo for the hapless Alain and Widow Simone's famous Clog Dance. The first performance was on 28 January 1960 at the Royal Opera House, Covent Garden.

Ashton was using the exceptional virtuosity of Nadia Nerina and David Blair, the first dancers to appear as the young lovers, Lise and Colas; the wonderful comic and pathetic gifts of Alexander Grant, the first Alain; and the great talents of Stanley Holden who brought a music-hall gusto to his characterisation of the Widow. The ballet is so well constructed, with its enchanting mixture of comedy and glorious classical dancing, that it has survived many casts and the characters themselves have become favourites with the ballet audience. Lise, in a different version, was one of Pavlova's great rôles. It is impossible to list all the Royal Ballet's Lises, but Merle Park, who followed Nerina, Doreen Wells, Ann Jenner and Lesley Collier, must be mentioned. As Colas, David Wall and Mikhail Baryshnikov are superb. The ballet is danced not only at Covent Garden but is also in the repertory of the Sadler's Wells Royal Ballet (shown here).

Act I

In a farmyard the dawn, heralded by the cockerel and his hens, sees Lise, only daughter of the wealthy Widow Simone, dreaming of Colas, the handsome, young farmer, she loves and hopes to marry. Lise picks up a ribbon and dances around the farmyard with it, expressing all the joy that fills her heart. As Lise goes into the outbuildings to begin work, in bounds the ebullient Colas in search of her. Unfortunately for Colas, he is chased away by the Widow Simone, who regards him as a penniless ne'er do well, and no suitable match for Lise.

Into the farmyard come the merry harvesters eager to complete their work. They leave for the fields and Simone sets Lise to churn butter, hoping to divert her thoughts from Colas. But, the moment Simone's back is turned, Colas creeps back. Lise dances with him, and again the ribbon features in their dance of joy and love. Colas departs as some farm girls arrive and Lise tells them of her secret love.

Widow Simone interrupts their excited chatter and sends the girls off to work. The mischievous Lise tries to slip out with them in order to rejoin Colas, but her mother catches her and is about to administer a good spanking when old farmer Thomas, a rich vineyard owner, comes into the farmyard with his simpleton son, Alain. Thomas and Simone plan to marry Alain to Lise, a good union commercially, but one with which Lise is far from happy as she witnesses Alain's idiotic antics.

They all set out for the fields to join the harvest-home celebrations, Simone and Lise in their little pony cart, and the dull-witted Alain happily scampering along behind.

Colas, not one to miss the chance of a party, makes his exuberant way to the fields with some wine to toast the harvest.

When Simone and Lise arrive the celebrations are in full swing. Colas enlists the aid of his friends, the farm girls and boys, to distract the giggling Alain while he cheekily steals a kiss from Lise. Colas and Lise slip away and dance a *pas de deux* celebrating their love, surrounded by their friends, whose bright pink ribbons flow into beautiful patterns as they dance.

Widow Simone discovers them, and in order to prevent her from venting her anger on the lovers, the harvesters persuade Simone to give them a display of clog dancing. This she does with great gusto, almost collapsing at the end and is much too tired to scold. A maypole is erected and the harvesters dance happily around it, with Lise and Colas at their centre. Suddenly, the skies darken, and, as the storm breaks, everyone, even Alain, runs for shelter.

Act II

Simone and Lise, soaked by the storm, return to the farmhouse. Hoping to keep Lise out of mischief, Simone asks her to help with the spinning. Almost at once Simone nods off to sleep and Lise, who has seen Colas outside, contrives to talk with him across the locked kitchen door. The knocking of the harvesters who have brought the sheaves from the field and now wish to be paid wakes Simone. Colas manages to creep into the room with them and hides among the sheaves. Simone takes the harvesters into the yard to give them a drink and to pay them, leaving Lise to her thoughts of the joys of marriage and children. Suddenly, to Lise's dismay, Colas springs out from his hiding place.

As Colas declares his love they hear Simone returning so Lise sends him to hide in her bedroom. Simone rushes in, sure that Colas has been there, but unable to prove it. She locks Lise in her room to prepare for the arrival of her bridegroom, Alain. The wedding guests enter followed by Thomas and Alain, and the marriage contract is signed before the notary. Simone gives Alain the key to Lise's door, but when he opens it there stand the lovers in each other's arms. Thomas furiously tears up the contract and leaves, closely followed by the despondent Alain.

Widow Simone is ashamed of the behaviour of her daughter and angry at the loss of a rich son-in-law. Lise and Colas beg her to let them marry, and all their friends add their pleas. Realising, finally, that she cannot stand in the way of true love, Widow Simone relents and gives her blessing. Lise and Colas are joyfully united at last among their rejoicing friends.

Giselle

Choreography: *Jean Coralli and Jules Perrot*. Music: *Adolphe Adam*.
Designs: *Peter Farmer*.

Cast. Giselle: *Antoinette Sibley*. Albrecht-Loys: *Anthony Dowell*. Hilarion:
David Gordon. Myrtha, Queen of the Wilis: *Deanne Bergsma*. Berthe:
Gerd Larsen. Bathilde: *Vergie Derman*

Peasants and Courtiers: *Artists of the Royal Ballet*.

Giselle (or *Les Wilis*) is the most important survival from the Romantic era in ballet which reached its heyday in the 1830s and 1840s. Ballet entered its Romantic phase with the production in 1832 at the Paris Opéra of *La Sylphide* which immortalised the great ballerina Marie Taglioni (1804–1884) and was the first ballet to make artistic use of the new discovery of dancing on full pointe – to suggest the flight of a supernatural being, the Sylphide. Charming though *La Sylphide* is, *Giselle* is a much more demanding and dramatically effective work.

The first production at the Paris Opéra on 28 June 1841 had a libretto by the poet Théophile Gautier who worked with the official librettist of the Paris Opéra, Vernoy de St. Georges, and its chief ballet master, Jean Coralli. Gautier took the story from a legend he had read in the writings of the German Heinrich Heine about the Wilis, ghostly maidens who rise from their graves at night and force any man they meet to dance himself to death. Coralli devised most of the group dances, but the choreography for Giselle herself was arranged by Jules Perrot, greatest male dancer and choreographer of his day. He was the lover of the first Giselle, Carlotta Grisi, and determined that her rôle should be a great one. The music, commissioned from Adolphe Adam, is wonderfully apt in the theatre and is an early example of theme tunes being given to the different characters. Giselle, happy then mad in the first act, ethereal in the second, did, as Perrot hoped, become one of the most cherished rôles for a ballerina. Grisi's successors included almost every great ballerina since her time. The rôle of Albrecht was created by Lucien Petipa (brother of Marius) and that too has been coveted over the years.

The success of *Giselle* swept Europe and in 1842 Perrot produced it in St. Petersburg. In Russia the ballet remained popular and there it was gradually enriched with a stronger technical element than Perrot would have known. Petipa's production of 1884 translated the ballet very much into the work which Sergueyev gave the Royal Ballet in 1934 with Markova and Dolin in the principal rôles, and which is seen lovingly preserved in Peter Wright's production today.

Act I

In a small cottage by a Rhineland forest, live a fair young maiden named Giselle, and her old mother, Berthe. There are two great loves in Giselle's life, dancing and Loys, a handsome country lad who lives in the hut opposite hers. Loys is, in reality, the Duke Albrecht, who, captivated by Giselle's beauty, has disguised himself in order to woo her. Hilarion, a woodcutter, also loves Giselle and suspects that Loys is not what he appears to be and that he is only toying with Giselle's affections.

One day, when Giselle and Loys are together by the forest, she picks a flower and plays a game of 'He loves me . . . he loves me not'. Giselle is upset when the last petal says 'He loves me not', and she cannot make it come out any other way. Loys takes the flower and pretends that it comes out as 'He loves me', and Giselle is reassured. The lovers are so absorbed that they do not notice Hilarion until he roughly separates them. He attacks Loys, warning him not to make love to Giselle, but Loys dismisses him.

Giselle is shaken by this angry scene, but is quickly cheered when her friends rush in and, with Loys, she leads them in a dance celebrating the successful conclusion of the grape harvest. Berthe enters and, worried that Giselle's dancing will cause her heart to fail, warns her daughter that if she dies she will become one of the Wilis, spirits doomed to dance for ever, even in death. But Giselle takes no notice and dances again. At the height of the merriment, Albrecht's squire warns him in an aside that a hunting party led by the Prince of Courland and his daughter Bathilde is approaching. Fearful of recognition, Albrecht withdraws and the hunting party enters. They stop for refreshment at Berthe's cottage and are served by Giselle who is fascinated by Bathilde's fine clothes. Giselle dances for Bathilde who gives her a beautiful necklace.

The hunting party enters the cottage to rest and Loys reappears and joins in the festivities which culminate with Giselle being crowned 'Queen of the harvest'. At the moment of Giselle's supreme happiness, the blow falls. Hilarion, who had seen Loys hide a cloak and sword in his hut, has stolen them and now shows them to Giselle as proof of Loy's deception.

Giselle does not believe that Loys is capable of such deceit, so Hilarion snatches up a hunting horn, and blows it, summoning the hunters from the cottage. Bathilde greets Loys as Albrecht, her fiancé, and Hilarion is proved right. When Giselle sees the ring on Bathilde's finger she is heartbroken. The sudden and brutal shock unbalances her mind and, oblivious to all around her, Giselle dances wildly, reliving her past happiness with Loys and she sees again the fateful game she played with him of 'He loves me . . . he loves me not'.

At this, the awful truth once more assails her deranged mind. Seizing Albrecht's sword she sweeps it madly around as the horrified onlookers shrink back.

Finally, her mental anguish too much to bear, Giselle throws herself onto the sword and dies in her mother's arms, leaving her friends grief-stricken, and both Albrecht and Hilarion aghast at the misery and disaster they have caused.

Act II

Deep in the forest, where Giselle lies buried, Hilarion comes to mourn at her graveside. He is afraid of encountering the Wilis, spirits of girls who have died before their wedding day who are sworn to dance to death any man they meet, and soon hurries away. Out of the night mist come the Wilis with their queen, Myrtha, who summons Giselle's spirit from the grave to join their ghostly ranks. A sudden noise disturbs the Wilis who melt back into the mist.

Albrecht enters bearing lilies to place on Giselle's grave. As he kneels in prayer at the graveside Giselle's spirit appears before him. At first Albrecht thinks he is dreaming and follows the ghost of his loved one into the forest. Just then Hilarion returns, only to be ensnared by Myrtha and the Wilis who drive him to his death. Albrecht and Giselle, unaware of Hilarion's death, enter once again.

The vengeful Wilis materialise and surround Albrecht, cutting off his path of escape. The awesome and terrible Myrtha, claiming another victim, condemns the Duke to dance until he dies of exhaustion. Giselle, in spite of all, still loves Albrecht and she joins him as he dances, willing him to survive. At last, when Albrecht is at the point of death, dawn breaks and Myrtha's power is dispelled. Having saved her lover's life, Giselle bids him a final farewell and returns to her mist-shrouded grave.

Romeo and Juliet

Choreography: *Kenneth MacMillan*. Music: *Serge Prokofiev*.
Scenery and costumes: *Nicholas Georgiadis*.

Cast. Romeo: *Rudolf Nureyev*. Juliet: *Margot Fonteyn*.
Mercutio: *David Blair*. Tybalt: *Desmond Doyle*. Benvolio: *Anthony Dowell*. Paris: *Derek Rencher*.
Lord Capulet: *Michael Somes*. Lady Capulet: *Julia Farron*. Escalus, Prince of Verona: *Leslie Edwards*.
Rosaline: *Georgina Parkinson*. Nurse: *Gerd Larsen*. Friar Laurence: *Ronald Hynd*.
Lord Montague: *Franklin White*. Lady Montague: *Betty Kavanagh*. Juliet's Friends: *Ann Howard,
Carole Hill, Ann Jenner, Jennifer Penney, Dianne Horsham, Virginia Wakelyn*.
Three Harlots: *Deanne Bergsma, Monica Mason, Carole Needham*. Mandolin Dance: *Keith Rosson,
Robert Mead, Ian Hamilton, Lambert Cox, Kenneth Mason, Austin Bennett*.
Ballroom Guests and townspeople: *Artists of the Royal Ballet*.

When the Bolshoy Ballet first appeared in London, at Covent Garden in 1956, they opened their season with Leonid Lavrovsky's ballet, *Romeo and Juliet*, with Galina Ulanova as Juliet – and they were a triumph. Lavrovsky had prepared the libretto, closely based on Shakespeare's play, in collaboration with Serge Prokofiev (1891–1953) the composer. This Soviet production, designed by Pyotr Williams, was first staged in Leningrad at the Kirov (formerly Maryinsky) Theatre on 11 January 1940 with Ulanova as Juliet. In 1946, Lavrovsky staged his ballet again in Moscow for the Bolshoy, but that magnificent version has since been replaced by a new one choreographed by the Bolshoy's director of ballet, Yuri Grigorovich. The libretto and the score have been used internationally as the basis for many different productions of the ballet. Prokofiev's music is marvellously theatrical, sonorous for the big dramatic scenes, soaring and lyrical for the love duets. The first Englishman to tackle this score was Frederick Ashton who made a beautiful version for the Royal Danish Ballet in 1955 – before the Soviet production had been seen in the West. Kenneth MacMillan's production, first produced by the Royal Ballet at Covent Garden on 9 February 1965, has established itself very firmly in the repertory and has been danced by many celebrated artists.

MacMillan created the role of Juliet for Lynn Seymour, the young Canadian dancer who has been his muse ever since he gave her the principal rôle in *The Burrow* (a ballet based on *The Diary of Anne Frank*) in 1958. Juliet is the strongest character in the ballet and dictates the action by the force of her passionate love for Romeo. The rôle of Romeo was written for Christopher Gable (now a successful actor) but the actual first performance (as shown in the following pages) was danced by Margot Fonteyn and Rudolf Nureyev. Many other dancers have shone in the two principal rôles: Sibley, Park, Makarova, Collier among the Juliets; Dowell, Eagling and Baryshnikov as Romeo. David Blair, who died tragically young in 1976, was the first Mercutio, and Desmond Doyle the first Tybalt in this production. Both are exciting parts and there are many smaller danced or mimed rôles which, together with the big group dances, make this MacMillan version one of the most successful to be seen anywhere today.

Act I

As dawn breaks in the market place of Verona, Romeo, son of Lord Montague, is trying, with little success, to woo Rosaline. His friends, Mercutio and Benvolio attempt to console him, and Romeo is soon drawn into the cheerful dancing. As the market square gradually fills with bustling activity, Tybalt enters with some friends. He is a Capulet, sworn enemies of the Montagues, and before long the two factions are exchanging taunts and jibes.

Tempers flare and a violent duel begins, in which the Lords Montague and Capulet themselves become embroiled. Trumpets herald the arrival of the Prince of Verona. Shocked at this barbarous display in the streets of his city, he orders the duellists to put up their swords and decrees that the family feuding must cease.

In an ante-room of the Capulet house, Juliet, the beautiful young daughter of Lord Capulet, is playing with her dolls, fondly supervised by her old nurse. Lord and Lady Capulet enter and present Juliet to Paris, a wealthy young nobleman who has asked for her hand in marriage. After they have left, the kind old nurse explains to Juliet that she is now too old for dolls and must act like a grown woman.

The Capulets are holding a ball at their palace to which Rosaline has been invited, but to which no Montague may go. To pursue his courtship of Rosaline, Romeo, together with his two friends, disguises himself in a mask and gains entry to the ball. At the height of the festivities, Juliet enters and dances first with Paris, then, with all the joy and exhuberance of a girl at her first ball, alone.

Romeo, his passion for Rosaline forgotten, is captivated by the freshness and beauty of Juliet, and as she sits playing the mandoline he dances before her to gain her attention. At last Romeo is able to dance alone with Juliet, only to be interrupted by Tybalt who recognises him and makes to throw him out. Lord Capulet however, mindful of the Prince of Verona's decree, restrains Tybalt and makes Romeo welcome in his house.

That night Juliet, her emotions in a turmoil, is unable to sleep. She comes out on to her balcony and sees Romeo in the garden below. She runs down into his arms. Hopelessly in love, they dance tenderly together under the night sky, until, at last Romeo must leave.

Act II
The market place next day is thronged with merry-makers as a wedding procession passes through. Romeo's friends join in the celebrations, but Romeo is still lost in dreams of marriage to Juliet. Juliet's old nurse arrives and pushes through the crowds with a letter for Romeo. With his friends, Romeo teases and confuses the old lady and finally he pretends to steal the letter and only then reveals his identity to the scandalised nurse who departs in a huff.

Act III

Romeo and Juliet have spent one night of love together, but as dawn breaks, Romeo knows he must leave before he is discovered. He tries to slip away to save them both the pain of parting, but Juliet wakes and rushes to him, unable to bear the thought of losing him. Romeo dances lovingly with his young bride.

Romeo, resolved to end the feud between Montague and Capulet, entreats Mercutio to stop. As he pleads with his friend, the enraged Tybalt makes another rush, stabs Mercutio in the back and kills him. In a blind rage at seeing his friend slain, Romeo snatches up Mercutio's sword and kills Tybalt. As Lady Capulet grieves over Tybalt's body, Benvolio persuades Romeo, who is now distraught at the implications of what he has done, to flee.

Shortly after, the lovers
meet at the chapel and
Friar Laurence blesses
their union, hoping that
their marriage will end
the strife between the
two families. Romeo
returns to the market
place only to find Tybalt
there, arguing with
Mercutio. A violent duel
begins with Mercutio
gaining the upper hand.

As his friends return to their revelry, Romeo opens and reads Juliet's letter. She has consented to become his wife and has proposed a secret marriage, that day at the chapel of Friar Laurence.

The ecstatic Romeo dances joyfully about the market place and rushes to keep the rendezvous.

Eventually, though loath to do so, the lovers must part as the house is stirring. Just as Romeo has climbed from the balcony and Juliet is still lost in the warmth of his last embrace, the nurse enters, followed by Juliet's parents and Paris.

Juliet's parents tell her that the time has come for her to marry Paris. Unable to tell them her secret, Juliet refuses to accept the match, greatly angering her father. She cannot bear the thought of being forced into Paris' arms and rejects his advances. Paris leaves, deeply hurt, and Lord Capulet threatens to disown Juliet unless she comes to her senses and marries Paris.

After they have left, Juliet snatches up her cloak and runs to seek help from Friar Laurence. He listens to her tale and gives her a sleeping potion which will induce a death-like sleep.

Thinking her dead, her parents will place her in the family vault and Romeo, forewarned by Friar Laurence, will come to take her away. That evening, Juliet's parents return with Paris and again try to make her agree to the match. Finally, she consents and her delighted parents leave with Paris.

Juliet opens the phial of sleeping draught and drains it. As drowsiness overcomes her, she falls on her bed. The next morning Juliet's bridesmaids enter to prepare her for the ceremony and find her seemingly dead. Her parents are grief stricken and her body is taken to the family tomb. Romeo, who has received no word from Friar Laurence, enters the tomb believing that his bride is dead. He finds Paris grieving for Juliet and kills him.

Overcome by grief Romeo picks up Juliet's still body and dances in tragic parody of their last meeting. He replaces her form on the bier and, with nothing left to live for, takes a phial of poison, and falls dead by her side. A few moments later, Juliet stirs and then awakens. She finds Romeo's body, and realises that Friar Laurence's plan has tragically miscarried and all is lost. Taking his dagger, she plunges it into her breast and dies, so that her soul and Romeo's may be united for ever.

The Sleeping Beauty

Choreography: *Marius Petipa after the 1939 production of Nicolai Sergueyev, with additional choreography by Frederick Ashton*. Production: *under the supervision of Ninette de Valois*. Music: *Pyotr Ilyich Tchaikovsky*. Designs: *David Walker*.

Cast. Princess Aurora: *Lesley Collier*. Prince Florimund: *Anthony Dowell*
Queen: *Rosalind Eyre*. King: *Anthony Conway*. Carabosse: *Lynn Seymour*.
Catalabutte: *Leslie Edwards*. Fairy of the Lilac: *Vergie Derman*.

Fairy of Crystal Fountain: *Marguerite Porter*. Fairy of the Enchanted Garden: *Wendy Ellis*.
Fairy of the Woodland Glades: *Alfreda Thorogood*. Fairy of the Song Birds: *Ann Jenner*.
Fairy of the Golden Vine: *Laura Connor*. Cavaliers: *Derek Deane, Stephen Beagley, Michael Batchelor, Andrew Moore, Ross MacGibbon, Julian Hocking*. Princes: *David Drew, Derek Rencher, Julian Hosking, Derek Deane*. Friends of Aurora: *Hilary Tickner, Denise Nunn, Susan Lockwood, Julie Lincoln, Bess Dales, Rosalyn Whitten, Belinda Corken, Anita Young*.
Countess: *Georgina Parkinson*. Puss-in-Boots & the White Cat: *Anita Young, Christopher Carr*.
Bluebirds: *Alfreda Thorogood, Michael Coleman*. Hop O' My Thumb: *Wayne Sleep*.
The Three Ivans: *Graham Fletcher, Garry Grant, Andrew Moore*.
Florestan and His Two Sisters: *Stephen Beagley, Wendy Ellis, Laura Connor*.

Dame Ninette de Valois, founder of the Royal Ballet, has always considered *The Sleeping Beauty* as the signature work of her company and it has seldom been out of the repertory since she first engaged Sergueyev to revive it on the tiny stage of Sadler's Wells Theatre in 1939. That was a modest production, but it retained much of the original choreography and gave the young Margot Fonteyn what was to become her greatest rôle, the Princess Aurora. When the Sadler's Wells (now the Royal) Ballet reopened the Royal Opera House, Covent Garden in 1946, *The Sleeping Beauty*, newly and handsomely designed by Oliver Messel, was the ballet which triumphantly brought the Opera House back to life.

The Sleeping Beauty was the greatest of the collaborations between Marius Petipa and Tchaikovsky and indeed the greatest ballet of the whole glorious epoch in Imperial Russia. The Director of the Imperial Theatres, I. A. Vsevolozhsky, based his ideas for the ballet on the fairy story by Perrault. Petipa's precise instructions to Tchaikovsky inspired the composer to write a score that is perfect for the choreography and thrillingly beautiful in its own right. The first performance was in January 1890 at the Maryinsky Theatre, St. Petersburg in the presence of the Emperor Alexander III and the whole court. The first full length production in the West was presented by the great Russian impresario and animator of ballet, Serge Diaghilev, at the Alhambra Theatre in London on 21 November 1921.

The rôle of Aurora, great testing piece of the grand ballerina style, was created by the Italian Carlotta Brianza and the first Russian to master the part was Mathilde Kchessinskaya (1872–1971). The famous teacher, Enrico Cecchetti, doubled as the wicked fairy, Carabosse, and the Blue Bird in 1890. (Both he and Brianza returned to the stage to play mime rôles in the Diaghilev revival.)

There have been many productions in the West since de Valois proved the importance of the ballet. The Royal Ballet tried two different stagings, in 1968 and 1973, before asking Dame Ninette to try, in the 1977 production (shown here), to get back to the Sergueyev version. This she has largely succeeded in doing, while retaining some Ashton choreography from other productions, notably the Garland Dance, Aurora's Vision Scene solo, the Florestan *pas de trois* and the considerable amount of extra dancing now given to the Prince. *The Sleeping Beauty*, in addition to its own greatness as a ballet is a wonderful work in which dancers can develop, from small but very demanding solos to the greatest of all ballerina rôles.

Prologue

King Florestan XXIV and his Queen make their entrance to receive the guests for the christening of their infant daughter, Aurora. The King reviews the guestlist drawn up by Catalabutte, his Master of Ceremonies, unaware as yet of a disastrous omission.

Six fairy godmothers arrive at the court to give their blessing to the royal child. Accompanied by their handsome cavaliers the beautiful fairies dance in celebration of the joyous event.

The most powerful fairy of them all is the Lilac Fairy, who spreads her blessing on the assembled court. The fairies, who have given their gifts to the Princess, dance in turn.

Suddenly the skies darken and the guests shrink back as, amid thunder and lightning, the wicked fairy, Carabosse enters with her familiar spirits. Carabosse has not been invited so, in revenge, she puts a curse on Aurora. When the child grows up she will prick her finger on a spindle and die! No one can lift the curse, but the Lilac Fairy lessens its effect. Aurora will not die, but she will fall asleep for a hundred years until awakened by the kiss of a Prince.

Act I

Twenty years pass without mishap as, fearful of the curse, the King has banned all sharp objects from the palace. It is Aurora's birthday and farm maidens entertain the court with a floral dance. The Princess is very beautiful and Princes from far and near have come to seek her hand in marriage. She dances the famous 'Rose Adagio' with her suitors, receiving a rose from each.

An old woman pushes forward with a gift for the Princess. It is a spindle! Aurora takes it, fascinated by the unfamiliar object. Before her horrified parents can snatch the spindle away from her Aurora pricks her finger and falls into a faint. The old woman casts off her disguise. It is Carabosse, who vanishes laughing with wicked delight. The Lilac Fairy appears to fulfil her promise. As Aurora and the whole court sink into a deep sleep, she hides the palace in an enchanted forest.

Act II

One hundred years later the handsome Prince Florimund and his companions are hunting, in the enchanted forest. The Prince, who is in a sad and pensive mood, soon wearies of the revelry and does not join the chase, but remains alone in the forest. Here, the Lilac Fairy appears to him and tells him of the Princess Aurora's plight, while revealing the beautiful princess to him in a vision.

Enchanted by Aurora's beauty, Florimund dances with the apparition conjured up by the Lilac Fairy. The wood nymphs of the enchanted forest join the vision and the Prince in their *pas de deux*, before both they and Aurora disappear.

Totally captivated, Florimund begs the Lilac Fairy to take him to the Sleeping Beauty and she wafts him to the palace in her fairy boat drawn by doves.

Act III
The Lilac Fairy guides Florimund through the slumbering palace to where Aurora sleeps. He kneels and kisses the Princess and she awakens. The curse is lifted, and, as the dark forest withdraws, the rest of the court wakes from its long and peaceful sleep. Aurora and Florimund dance joyfully together and declare their love.

It is Aurora and Florimund's wedding day and a great celebration has been arranged. Catalabutte receives the fairy-tale characters who are to dance at the festivities; among them are Puss-in-Boots and the White Cat. The Bluebird soars and leaps to the delight and amazement of the court in his brilliant *divertissement*.

Florimund and Aurora express their joy at their marriage in an exuberant *pas de deux*. The entertainment is then brought to a lively end by the three Ivans who perform an exhilarating Cossack dance. The bounty of the Lilac Fairy has triumphed over the machinations of the wicked Carabosse and the Prince and Princess live happily ever after.